F.C. BAYERN MUNICH

By

Mark Stewart

NORWOODHOUSE PRESS

Chicago, Illinois

NORWOOD HOUSE ![logo] PRESS

P.O. Box 316598 • Chicago, Illinois 60631
For more information about Norwood House Press please visit our website at
www.norwoodhousepress.com or call 866-565-2900.

Photography and Collectibles:
The trading cards and other memorabilia assembled in the background for this book's cover and interior pages
are all part of the author's collection and are reproduced for educational and artistic purposes.

All photos courtesy of Associated Press except the following individual photos and artifacts (page numbers):
Golden Wonder Ltd. (6), F.K.S. Publishers Ltd. (10 top), Edizioni Panini (10 bottom),
Rafo/Mostar (11 top, middle), Panini SpA (11 bottom, 16), Juego del 5 (22).

Cover image: Emilio Morenatti/Associated Press

Designer: Ron Jaffe
Series Editor: Mike Kennedy
Content Consultants: Michael Jacobsen and Jonathan Wentworth-Ping
Project Management: Black Book Partners, LLC
Editorial Production: Lisa Walsh

LIBRARY OF CONGRESS CATALOGING-IN-PUBLICATION DATA
Names: Stewart, Mark, 1960 July 7- author.
Title: F.C. Bayern Munich / By Mark Stewart.
Description: Chicago Illinois : Norwood House Press, 2017. | Series: First
   Touch Soccer | Includes bibliographical references and index. | Audience:
   Age 5-8. | Audience: K to Grade 3.
Identifiers: LCCN 2016058200 (print) | LCCN 2017005789 (ebook) | ISBN
   9781599538570 (library edition : alk. paper) | ISBN 9781684040766 (eBook)
Subjects: LCSH: FC Bayern (Soccer team)--History--Juvenile literature.
Classification: LCC GV943.6.F36 S74 2017 (print) | LCC GV943.6.F36 (ebook) |
   DDC 796.334/640943364--dc23
LC record available at https://lccn.loc.gov/2016058200

302N--072017
Manufactured in the United States of America in North Mankato, Minnesota.

CONTENTS

Words in **bold type** are defined on page 24.

Philipp Lahm congratulates Arjen Robben after a goal in a 2016 match.

Meet F.C. Bayern Munich

Munich is the third-largest city in Germany. Its most popular soccer team is Fussball Club Bayern Munich. Bayern is German for Bavaria, which is the largest state in Germany. When people say "fussball" in Germany they are talking about the game of soccer, not American football.

Bayern fans call their club Die Roten, which is German for The Reds. The players wear their red uniforms with great pride and play with amazing skill.

The Bayern Munich soccer team started as part of a gymnastics club. From 1900 until the 1970s, the club went through many ups and downs. This included two World Wars. Bayern was the best club in Europe during the mid-1970s. It has been a soccer power ever since. Its great players include **Sepp Maier**, Paul Breitner, Karl-Heinz Rummenigge and Stefan Effenberg.

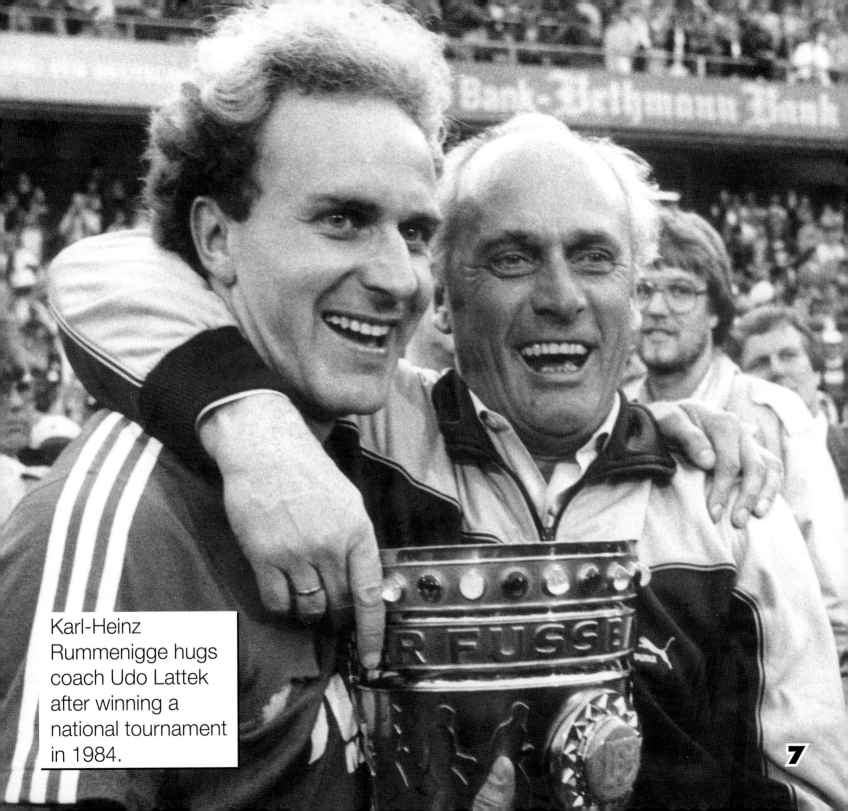

Karl-Heinz Rummenigge hugs coach Udo Lattek after winning a national tournament in 1984.

A computer network controls the LED lights around the club's stadium.

BEST SEAT IN THE HOUSE

Bayern Munich plays its home matches in Germany's second-largest stadium. It was the first stadium that could change colors on the outside. It is beautiful at night. Bayern shares its field with another club in the city, TSV 1860 Munich. Bayern and TSV are both members of the Bundesliga, which is German for Federal League.

COLLECTOR'S CORNER

These collectibles show some of the best Bayern players ever.

FRANZ BECKENBAUER

Defender

1964–1977

Beckenbauer was nicknamed "The Emperor." He was always the top man on the field.

GERD MULLER

Striker

1964–1979

Muller had one of the hardest shots in history. Fans called him "The Bomber."

LOTHAR MATTHAUS

LOTHAR MATTHAUS

Midfielder/Defender
1984–1988 & 1992–2000
Matthaus seemed to be everywhere on the field at once. He played for Germany in five **World Cups**.

OLIVER KAHN

OLIVER KAHN

Goalkeeper
1994–2008
Kahn had the size and quickness of an American football player. He led Bayern to eight league championships.

FRANCK RIBERY

2013
Franck Ribéry
FIFA 365

Forward/Midfielder
First Year with Club: 2007
Ribery amazed fans when he joined the team. He is one of the best in the world at dribbling, passing, and shooting.

WORTHY OPPONENTS

Bayern Munich's main rival is Borussia Dortmund. The two clubs are always among the best in the country. In 2013, they met in the final of the Champions League, Europe's biggest tournament. Bayern won, 2–1. Bayern also has a rivalry with F.C. Nurnberg, which plays in Nuremberg, Germany.

Arjen Robben out-jumps Dortmund's Marcel Schmelzer for a header in the 2013 Champions League final.

CLUB WAYS

Many people think of Bayern Munich as "Germany's Team." More than 10 million Germans say they are Bayern fans. Another 10 million around the world say they are fans, too. Bayern has more than 3,000 fan clubs in Germany alone. Wherever the team plays, club members buy up as many tickets as they can.

The players celebrate with their fans after a match in Mainz, Germany. Bayern Munich has supporters in every German city.

ON THE MAP

Bayern brings together players from many countries. These are some of the best:

1 **Johnny Hansen** • Vejle, Denmark

2 **David Alaba** • Vienna, Austria ●

3 **Arjen Robben** • Bedum, Netherlands

4 **Hasan Salihamidzic**
   Jablanica, Bosnia and Herzegovina

5 **Samuel Osei Kuffour** • Kumasi, Ghana

6 **Claudio Pizarro** • Callao, Peru

7 **Giovane Elber** • Londrina, Brazil

8 **Martin Demichelis** • Justiniano, Argentina

MAP OF EUROPE

Bayern's home stadium is in Munich, Germany.

WORLD MAP

Thomas Muller wears the club's home kit during a 2016 game.

KIT AND CREST

Bayern Munich's uniform has used a shade of red for more than 100 years. The home uniform has been mostly red since the mid-1970s. The club's away **kit** has changed many times. Bayern has worn black, blue, white, gold, and green as the visiting team. The club's crest show's the blue and white colors of Bavaria.

WE WON!

For three years in the 1970s, Bayern Munich was one of the greatest clubs ever. Franz Beckenbauer, Gerd Muller, Sepp Maier, and Uli Hoeness led the team to three **European Cup** finals. They beat Atletico Madrid in 1974. They beat Leeds United in 1975. They won again in 1976, defeating A.C. Saint-Etienne. Only two other clubs have won three times in a row.

Gerd Muller (right) watches his diving header find the net in the 1974 European Cup final. Muller scored twice in Bayern Munich's 4–0 victory.

FOR THE RECORD

Bayern Munich has won more than 50 major championships!

Bundesliga

25 championships
(from 1968–69 to 2015–16)

European Cup/Champions League

1973–74   2000–01
1974–75   2012–13
1975–76

Cup Winners' Cup

1966–67

Club World Cup

2013

German Cup

18 championships
(from 1956–57 to 2015–16)

Intercontinental Cup

1976
2001

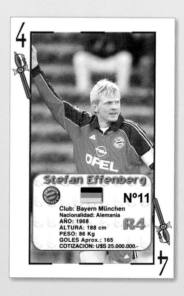

Stefan
Effenberg

These stars won major awards while playing for Bayern Munich:

1970 Gerd Muller • European Footballer of the Year

1972 Franz Beckenbauer • European Footballer of the Year

1976 Franz Beckenbauer • European Footballer of the Year

1980 Karl-Heinz Rummenigge • European Footballer of the Year

1981 Karl-Heinz Rummenigge • European Footballer of the Year

1991 Lothar Matthaus • World Player of the Year

2001 Stefan Effenberg • Club Footballer of the Year

1999 Oliver Kahn • Goalkeeper of the Year

2000 Oliver Kahn • Goalkeeper of the Year

2001 Oliver Kahn • Goalkeeper of the Year

2002 Oliver Kahn • Goalkeeper of the Year

2013 Franck Ribery • European Footballer of the Year

Soccer Words

European Cup
An annual tournament among the top clubs in Europe. It is now called the Champions League.

Kit
The official league equipment of soccer players, including a club's uniform.

World Cups
The soccer tournaments held every four years open to teams of all nations.

Index

Photos are on **BOLD** numbered pages.

About the Author

Mark Stewart has been writing about world soccer since the 1990s, including *Soccer: A History of the World's Most Popular Game.* In 2005, he co-authored Major League Soccer's 10-year anniversary book.

About F.C. Bayern Munich

Learn more at these websites:
fcbayern.com/us
www.fifa.com
www.teamspiritextras.com